The Affirmation Handbook:
An Energy Charged Path to Growth

Antoinette Spurrier

You are a creator of possibilites and an adventurer on a journey. Your power of intention, imagination, affirmation, and your capacity to dream are your tools to create a life of true happiness aligned with your Higher Self.

© 2012 by Antoinette Spurrier. All rights reserved.

No part of this book may be reproduced, stored in a retrieval system, or transmitted by any means without the written permission of the author.

First published by Antoinette Spurrier through Lightening Source July 2012

ISBN: 978-0-9856857-5-1 (hc)
ISBN: 978-0-9856857-4-4 (sc)
ISBN: 978-0-9856857-5-0 (ebk)

Library of Congress Control Number: 2012944135

Printed in the United States of America

Because of the dynamic nature of the Internet, any web addresses or links contained in this book may have changed since publication and may no longer be valid. The views expressed in this work are solely those of the author and do not necessarily reflect the views of the publisher, and the publisher hereby disclaims any responsibility for them.

Dedication

*This book is dedicated to my friends and family.
Knowing them affirms my life.*

Table of Contents

Introduction   1

Chapter One: The What and Why of Affirmations   3

Chapter Two: Power Charging Your Affirmations   24

Chapter Three:
Affirmations Change Consciousness   42

Chapter Four:
An Anthology of Spiritually Based Affirmations   58

Chapter Five: Thoughts for the Day: A Sampler   76

Acknowledgements

Collaborators:

Andrew Freedman
Editor, graph maker, friend and preserver of the intention. Andrew was the original inspiration for a mini-book series evolving from *Deliberate Happiness*.

Jacqui Freedman
Artistic contributor whose gift is the capturing of Spirit and Nature in her light-filled watercolors. Her work is available at Jacquifree@yahoo.com.

Heidi Hall
Co-editor of the primary *Deliberate Happiness* book. This edition, *The Affirmation Handbook*, is also graced by her inspirational input.

Becky Lawton
Initial contributor and administrative assistant for *Deliberate Happiness*.

Deborah Probst Kayes
Friend extraordinaire, copy editor, proofreader, coordinator and multi-tasker with extraordinary tenacity, patience and loyalty; bestower of tranquility in non-tranquil moments.

Suresh Ramaswamy
Creative website master for www.FieldsOfLight.com.

Jeffrey Spurrier
Professional writer, vital team member who assisted in important ways to the manifestation of this book.

Ann Summa
Photographer, soul sister, provider of proofreading and formatting expertise, as well as moral support for the *Deliberate Happiness* series.

Anne Marie Welsh
Co-editor and dynamic catalyst for the birthing process of *The Affirmation Handbook*. The "Book Doc" has allowed the creativity to shine abundantly inspired by the Indian goddess of the arts, Saraswati.

Contributors:

Family and friends who have provided love and moral support in magnanimous ways.

The Foundation for Spiritual and Personal Empowerment that provided the funding resources for the printing and distribution of the Deliberate Happiness book series.

Please refer to www.FieldsOfLight.com for more information.

Special Mention:

Sheila Byrne
Susann and Richard Fishman
Catherine Helm
Patrick McNabb
Deirdre and Lou Maher
Wayne Mantyla
Geoffrey and Sandra Mavis
Dr. Carl and Chris Murphy
Mark Murphy
Lisa Janicek Scurr and Ron Scurr

Introduction

To the Reader,

The Affirmation Handbook: An Energy Charged Path to Growth is the fourth installment in my series that began with *Deliberate Happiness, Practical Steps to an Empowered Life.* This shorter work distills certain themes from the main book into a discussion and exercises to ignite the power of spiritualized affirmations to change your habits of consciousness and thereby change your life.

I invite you to tap into your own habits of thought, and then, through introspection and practice, bring about fundamental changes in consciousness. These changes will allow you to charge your affirmations with full conviction and, in time, to manifest the blessings you deserve for your life and work. When properly applied, affirmations and meditation can lead to personal and spiritual empowerment, to powerful transformation and growth.

This book on the power of affirmations is not meant to replace the larger book, *Deliberate Happiness,* which analyzes the background of these practices and explains the natural patterns and scientific laws governing psychological and spiritual growth. In this smaller volume I focus on a sequence of techniques and ideas that, with patience and persistence, will bring the results described. The techniques include:

- Spiritual practices, including meditation, visualizations, journaling, introspection and especially affirmations, energized by the application of will.
- Methods of confronting deservedness issues by uprooting negative self-talk and altering long-standing feelings of worthlessness that sabotage love and happiness.

- A realistic focus on the power of affirmations to help overcome negative thoughts and behaviors.

My intention is to assist you in claiming the most of yourself. As you better understand spiritual law and these techniques, you will eventually return to your natural state of happiness, on the path to joy.

Antoinette Spurrier
San Diego, California

Chapter One

The What and Why of Affirmations

You are invited to align with spiritual truth through affirmations that will propel you along the path to deliberate happiness.

Properly understood and applied, spiritualized affirmations assist us in personal and spiritual empowerment and transformation. By affirming ideas that reflect spiritual truth, we align with that truth and deepen our self-knowing. This helps us manifest greater happiness.

Key topics addressed in this chapter:

- What are affirmations? Exploration and clarification.
- Are affirmation techniques for you?
- Journaling, and journaling exercise, for greater self-knowledge.
- Meditation techniques combined with affirmation techniques: the powerful duo that can power-charge your life.
- A short course on meditation.
- How to practice affirmations.

Affirmations Defined

Affirmations can power-charge your life, if you will take this adventure of discovery. In everyday speech, we may use the word "affirm" simply to denote "yes" or a larger positive assertion of one's ideas or one's self. Most use the word as described in Webster's Dictionary: "1: confirm 2: to assert positively 3: to make a solemn and formal declaration or assertion in place of an oath."

Affirmations as used here, however, apply to a specific technique based on spiritual and scientific principles that allows for a heightened level of alignment of our consciousness with Spirit. This alignment allows us to tap into the very force of creation and claim more of our true nature. By stating an affirmation, we claim our nature in words and then these energized words penetrate and expand in deeper recesses of self-knowing. Affirmations used properly have the power to activate more of our spiritual potency. Through the faithful and correct practice of affirmations, we align ourselves to the truth of our own spiritual nature. An affirmation creates a spiritualized force field expressed in words, with energy, movement and momentum.

> *By stating an affirmation, we claim our nature in words and then these energized words penetrate and expand in deeper recesses of self-knowing.*

Affirmations thus start a

potent vibration which corresponds to both a specific energy frequency and a state of consciousness in seed form. Over time, the affirmation begins to override other smaller vibrations which eventually become absorbed by the affirmation. Affirmations become power-charged by our focused attention and application of will-based energy.

Key General Concepts about Affirmations

Affirmations are an effective technique for change if we desire to:

- Change circumstances in our lives to a more positive outcome.
- Unleash our creative power by the dynamic force of intention.
- Create new possibilities in our lives.
- Explore new talents and new dimensions of ourselves.
- Heighten the beneficial use and power of imagination, visualization, and other life-altering techniques.
- Stop negative self-talk and uproot negative tenacious thought patterns that limit our happiness.
- Deepen spiritual life by exploring and expanding consciousness.

Principles Behind Affirmations

- They assist in creating new possibilities in any part of our lives.
- They deepen the energy blueprint in creation and stir movement toward manifestation of the desired outcome.
- Creation manifests from energized, repetitive affirmations.
- They increase our ability to develop willpower and discipline.
- Because energy seeks its vibrational counterpart, affirmations seek likeness through magnetic attraction or magnetic repulsion.
- They improve our conditions and circumstances, as **we affirm and visualize** changed circumstances in a positive, powerful manner. Affirmations thus become charged with our **activated will**. Creation manifests through this dynamic process, for the power of creation resides in our innate nature.
- Good has the power to continue to create and recreate, operating through the law of magnetic attraction: like attracts like. As we change our visualizations and utilize affirmations, we exercise our imagination. We change the energy we exude and that which is attracted to us by

our energy also shifts. In that energy change, new potency is created and new creation is manifesting.

Change your Thoughts, Change your Life

As we change our thoughts, we change our energy. As we change our energy, that which is attracted to us changes.

That truth is spiritual law in operation. No matter what our conditions, we have the power to redefine them. No matter what our situation, we have the power to visualize something different and something new. No matter what our circumstances, our power to co-create with the universe is amplified by our participation with it. We are potent co-creators of Divine possibilities and new discoveries. Our nature as energized love and light is in search of the highest vibration of itself.

Affirmations are a true and valid tool of consciousness transformation. Their power resides not only in the capacity to positively

> *"The brain is made up of tiny nerve cells called 'neurons'. These neurons have tiny branches that reach out and connect to other neurons to form a neural net. Each place where they connect is incubated into a thought or a memory. Now, the brain builds up all its concepts by the law of associative memory. For example, ideas, thoughts and feelings are all constructed and interconnected in this neural net and all have a possible relationship with one another."*
> "What the Bleep Do We Know?"
> -William Arntz, Betsy Chasse, Mark Vicente

impact the Limited Self, that part of us existing in a material world subject to decay and death. Affirmations also allow for greater self-integration by creating a bridge between our diverging selves—Limited and Eternal. They also promote alignment, coordination, attunement, and harmonious cooperation between the two selves.

To understand any resistance to transformation that we may encounter, we first must understand our own dual nature as both a Limited Self and an Eternal Self. These selves are in frequent communication and yet function in nearly opposite ways. This is not an abstract philosophical quandary; it is a reality. The Limited Self is identified and bound by a person's physical form, mind, feelings and culture. The other, the Eternal Self, expresses our spiritual nature, our true unchangeable essence.

The Limited Self has four aspects: our biological nature, operating in the physical dimension; our psychological layers of mental consciousness, operating within a social context; our beliefs and life experiences, operating within our environment and culture; and our imagination that can interpret and assign meaning to our experiences. The Limited Self may feel compartmentalized, incorrectly interpreting experiences and events, convinced of that which we wrongly imagine ourselves to be: body-identified and impermanent.

Our other Self, the expansive Eternal Self, is our true spiritual nature; its state of consciousness is transcendent joy. That Self, our soul nature, is aware of the actions of the Limited Self and manifests in subtle ways as an expression of who we truly are. Freely exercising our creativity can create a bridge linking Limited and Eternal, creating alignment and harmonious cooperation between them. Exercising our creative imaginations can put us in touch with the Divine Flow of creativity, actually making us co-Creators with the Divine.

Affirmations also alter energy and thought patterns. Our habitual attitudes form neural circuits in the brain. By choosing different habitual thoughts, we rewire the brain, creating new pathways to form new attitudes about ourselves or our relationships.

Donald Olding Hebb, the father of neuropsychology and author of *The Organization of Behavior*, wrote extensively on the function of neurons, or nerve cells, and how they contribute to psychological processes. His theory is often summarized as, *"cells that fire together, wire together."* This firing and wiring takes place in the synapses between neurons where information (communication) is transferred. The latest research indicates that memories and beliefs are stored in the neurons.

Effective affirmations from our conscious mind can and do reprogram (rewire) our nonconscious or subconscious mind. Over time, we will find that affirmations, combined with imagination, can change our faulty self-definitions. Affirmations can free up energy to conceive and define ourselves in new and life-enhancing ways. This unleashes tremendous power in us which naturally influences our lives, our creativity, and our relationships with others.

How Do Affirmations Change and Transform Your Life?

Affirmations energized with commitment can:

1. Change your mental habits of negativity to positive claiming.
2. Change your habits of emotional reactivity. We create habits of feeling and reaction by associating emotions with events. The repetition of associated ideas and feelings ingrains habits of reaction.
3. Change the mental energy grooves in the brain itself, for the neural net patterns themselves can be altered.
4. Change habits of thinking around worthiness and deservedness. Habits and feeling states around a lack of deservedness can damage every vital area of life.
5. Integrate diverging aspects of the finite self, here referred to as the Limited Self. Power-charging

your life can be accomplished by the systematic use of affirmations. They are tools of change and transformation.

Journaling To Discover Who We Truly Are

When we approach journaling with an open mind and heart, and we commit to being completely candid with ourselves, we open up to limitless opportunity for growth and healing. Through total honesty, we begin to peel away the layers of our psyche. The masks we wear begin to fall away, revealing our true nature - who we are when we aren't, "the parent, the employee, the friend," and are just ourselves.

Christin Synder, *The Healing Power of Journaling*

A helpful step toward effective affirmations and a key tool in the transformation of consciousness, journaling can help unlock the mind and open the heart. When we fully reveal ourselves, we can then affirm ideas that will truly place us on the road to happiness and joy. Journaling allows us to focus on our habits in consciousness and to identify the areas we need to change. It allows us to proceed with depth and clarity.

The habit of journaling not only leads to greater awareness of ourselves, but can create a journey map that, in the end, leads to self-discovery. Journaling can both clarify ideas and open fresh windows of introspection. When we journal honestly, deeply and regularly, we employ a powerful tool on our journey of discovery. Asking tough questions and writing down answers may allow us to go deeper into self-understanding instead of remaining at a superficial level of ideas about ourselves.

If we are to use spiritualized affirmations to create more happy and abundant lives and become a more effective co-creator with the universe, then we need to explore our personal perspective on the subject of happiness. Journaling is a way to see our attitudes, expectations, and feelings about happiness. By writing an inventory of our present state of happiness, we begin a central dialogue that lets us create a baseline to assess our growth and capacity for that state of mind which makes it possible to achieve enduring happiness.

You are invited to do these journal exercises in the spirit of self-discovery. You may be in a state of perfect health, and have abundant opportunities and meaningful relationships, but you may still feel unhappy or dissatisfied. You may also see happiness as a goal of the future, unattainable in the present. Danger lurks in always thinking, "I will be happy later." That becomes an affirmation in which we are telling ourselves, "Don't be happy now. You can't be happy now. Be happy later." Such ideas poison the Now. The

Now is all we have and all we will ever have in life, if only we knew it.

Journaling Activity: Are You Happy Now?

Write down your present feelings about being emotionally fulfilled and possessing inner contentment.
- Is your daily frame of mind peace and joy-filled?
- How much is your happiness tied to the past?
- How much is tied to the future?
- How much is tied to career?
- How much are expectations around others?
- Is your idea of happiness tied to a future expectation?
- Is happiness in your life on the installment plan?

If you answered yes to the last two questions, you might ask yourself how many years do you believe it will take for a desired accomplishment to happen? Do you assume that contentment, inner satisfaction, and happiness will be the result?

Finally, you might ask whether your desire to acquire or possess in any way violates the well being, or the happiness, of another person?

Penetrate into the Stillness: A Short Course on Meditation

If the doors of perception were cleansed, everything would appear to us as it is, Infinite.
William Blake

Meditation is another crucial technique which will assist you in power-charging your affirmation practice. In fact, even more than journaling, meditation is fundamental to any deep changes in consciousness, and to any life change. By meditating, all people — no matter how fearful, violent or lost—can open themselves to the sacred within and become free. Meditation allows us access to the deeper regions of our spiritual nature, connects us with the Divine presence within, and provides us a clearer vision of the truth. Positive affirmations are truth uttered in sound.

Scheduling time each day for meditation practice is essential not only for peace and well-being, but for discovering the Self. Interiorized consciousness allows access to your spiritual nature. This practice along with journaling enhances the results of will-based affirmations and can bring us toward experiencing our Eternal Selves, the true source of lasting happiness. However, affirmations should not be suspended until the journaling and meditation practices are mastered. We need to begin to chisel our way toward forming new thoughts in order to reveal the masterpiece of who we truly are. The key to maximizing progress with affirmations is to commit to the path to success in the beginning. My poem describes that journey:

Leap-Frogging Mind

Mind, Mind
Splintering, leaping mind
Unite with the breath
Of being.

Mind, Mind
Leap frogging player
Plumb the depths of
Your cavern of Knowing.

Mind, Mind
Dissolve your restless frenzy
The net of peace
Shall catch you
Tenderly.

Mind, Mind
Go beyond that Lily pad
Of distraction
Serenity beacons, joy awaits.

Mind, Mind
Consciousness supreme,
The net of peace
Shall catch you
Tenderly.

There are countless meditation techniques available and myriad philosophies about the proper method of meditation. Finding an effective and suitable style of meditation may take time, but will prove invaluable.

Note: Highly effective, balanced meditation techniques are available from Self-Realization Fellowship in the form of lessons that are delivered to your home every two weeks. For information contact:

> Self-Realization Fellowship
> 3880 San Rafael Drive
> Los Angeles, CA 90065-3219
> 323-225-2471
> http//www.yogananda-srf.org

One technique that will bring consistent results is offered below. This technique has some similarities to a Self-Realization Fellowship method but is not connected with or based on the work of that organization.

Meditation Technique

The proper posture for meditation is very important:

- Sitting in a straight back chair is recommended.
- The feet should be on the floor or flat surface, pointed straight ahead.
- In a state of relaxation, maintain a straight spine to the best of your ability without straining or discomfort.
- Place your hands, with palms turned gently upward, near the junction between your legs and thighs, or hands may be turned upward and placed slightly lower on the upper thighs.
- Note: Meditation techniques, in general, should not be practiced in a position where the individual is lying down in a bed. When lying down, the meditative state too easily becomes a sleep state. If an individual has the physical

ability to sit either in a chair with feet flat on the floor or cross-legged on the floor on a flat surface, the sitting posture should be assumed. In general, avoid sitting on a bed, for consciousness usually associates the bed with sleep.

This meditation technique involves focusing your attention at the point between the eyebrows known as the "third eye" or spiritual eye. This is a center that increases our spiritual connectedness as we focus upon it. If you are having difficulty in achieving or maintaining the proper eye position for your meditation, the following suggestion may assist you in getting the correct angle for your focus gaze. The eyes should be turned gently and slightly upward.

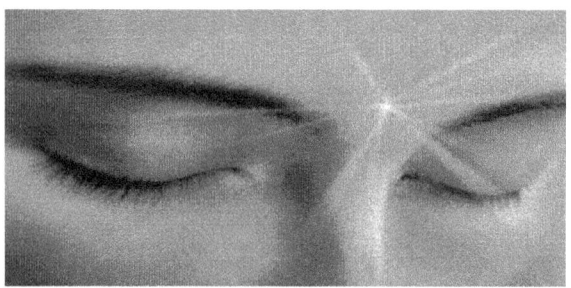

Pencil Technique for Proper Gaze

Visualize holding a #2 pencil eraser at the spiritual eye. (See diagram.) Visualize the eraser resting on the forehead between and slightly above the eyebrows, centered at the spiritual eye. The pencil should be parallel to the floor. Allow your focus to move to where you visualize the point of the pencil to be. Keep the gaze focused at that spot. This technique is not part of the practice itself, but is a tool that will prevent you from placing excessive strain on the eyes and help develop a better habit pattern for meditation.

Note: There should be no strain or tension. This is a natural, pleasant position for the eyes.

Preparation for Meditation:

- Visualize that you are encircled by white light which either outlines the body or is shaped in a spherical egg-shape. It is the **intention** to place white light around the body that summons a greater connection with Spirit and strengthens the energy field.

- After visualizing the white light in this way, begin to observe the breath in a relaxed state of mind. Maintain the correct posture with spine erect and feet flat on the floor.

- Affirm that you are divinely protected by the surrounding white light of Spirit. (Example: "I am surrounded by the light field of the Divine. I am ever protected. I am ever embraced by the Divine Force.") Repeat this protection affirmation, or a similar one, from 12-16 times.

- Now, in this relaxed state of mind, begin to observe the breath without any attempt to regulate it. Neither speed up nor slow down the rhythm of the breath. Simply observe the inhalation and exhalation as it naturally flows in and out.

- See yourself as "piggy-backing" on each inhalation and exhalation. Mentally say, "I ride the inward breath." As you naturally begin to exhale, mentally say, "I ride the outward breath." Continue this pattern for approximately 15 minutes. Visualize yourself riding the inward breath and the outward breath. Then change the repetition of words on the inhaling and exhaling breath to, "I am That[1]".

Additional affirmations may be mentally repeated prior to or following the use of this meditation technique:

I ride the inward breath.
I ride the outward breath.
I am one with that breath. Reveal Thyself.

You will accelerate your ability to penetrate stillness if, for three weeks, you practice meditation, journaling and these other components of your ritual of transformation every day:

- **Meditating for a minimum of 10 minutes.**
- **Journaling for 15 minutes on this theme.**

---
[1] "I am That" refers to our being One with the Indwelling Spirit.

- **Positive introspection.**
- **Holding a Thought for the Day.**
- **Repeating One or More Affirmations.**

Your thought for the day will likely be a simple truth such as this one from Mother Theresa, "If you judge people, you have no time to love them." Or perhaps it will be a more complex thought such as this one from the great Irish poet, W. B. Yeats: "We can make our minds so like still water that beings gather about us that they may see, it may be, their own images and so live for a moment with a clearer, perhaps even with a fiercer life because of our quiet."

Or you may wish to ponder a poem on the theme of stillness and tranquility. Here is a good one by Wendell Berry:

Go Among Trees and Sit Still

I go among trees and sit still.
All my stirring becomes quiet
Around me like circles on water.
My tasks lie in their places
Where I left them, asleep like cattle...
Then what I am afraid of comes.
I live for a while in its sight.
What I fear in it leaves it,
And the fear of it leaves me.
It sings, and I hear its song.

Many other thoughts for the day are included in the final section of the book, Chapter Five.

During the meditation portion of your practice, you may also choose an affirmation to begin the practice or to intensify your focus with a spiritually centered thought. Repeat it over mentally five or six times to help you maintain focus. Here are two possibilities:

I mount
the incoming breath.
I ride to the end.
I let the breath
begin its descent
while I mount for the
downward ride.
I ride the breath
of mind.

Or

Still lake of peace,
I drink tranquility.
I sip waters of knowing.
I penetrate the stillness.

While you may begin the meditation practice by the repetition of affirmations, do not continue them when in the interiorized meditative state itself. The restless mind is always attempting to re-energize the meditator. To bring the affirmations again during a state of calm interiorized consciousness can re-engage the leap-frogging mind and disrupt the depth being achieved.

My Name was the Name of All

I affirm my essence.
I affirm my being.
My words spoke the truth of who I am.

I am that essence.
I am that creator.
I am that being.

I affirm my essence.
I affirm my being.
My name is the name of All.

As I called my name
My essence emerged
Into powerful form
From the field of light.

As I called my name
I beheld the truth:
The field of light
was my own.

A Daily Ritual or Sadhana

If meditation is already a part of your daily practice or, once it has become comfortable for you, it is wise to continue practicing all the elements that can bring you closer and deeper into your true self, your spiritual consciousness. Repetition accelerates foundational change, establishing new patterns of thought that other activities such as reading cannot create. By revolving new positive thoughts in your mind, you will create new energy grooves in your brain.

As noted above, during this process of reprogramming, your day should include:

- **Meditating for ten minutes or more.**
- **Journaling for fifteen minutes.**
- **A thought for the day.**
- **A spiritualized affirmation.**

Write your chosen affirmation on five 3x5 file cards. Place those cards over your desk, on your bathroom mirror, above the kitchen sink, on your car dashboard—where ever you are most likely to see the card and thus be reminded to say the affirmation again. You may speak it out loud or mentally, depending upon circumstances. Aim for fifteen repetitions each day. This daily practice should become the heart of your effort to systematically begin to create change.

Chapter Two

Power-Charging Your Affirmations

You are invited to empower yourself by power-charging your affirmations with repetition, intention, clarity and consistency.

You have the innate capacity to experience joy now! That capacity is tied to affirming from the deepest and truest part of your own nature. It is tied to the essence of who you are!

Key Topics addressed in this chapter:

- How to power-charge your affirmations.
- How to create, and practice, spiritualized affirmations.
- Energized ideas, with power-filled intention and dynamic willpower, create fields of attraction and possibilities of manifestation.
- Spiritualized affirmations can result in permanent positive transformation.
- How to create and practice spiritualized affirmations.

- Spiritualized affirmations are a technique for personal transformation.
- Spiritualized affirmations, properly done, rewire the cognitive map of the brain. Positive repetition of ideas actually changes the biochemical physiology of the brain. As ideas change in energized ways, we transform ourselves.

How to Charge Your Affirmations

Once you have developed the capacity to meditate, to cultivate a daily practice, and become open to spiritual consciousness, your affirmations will become even more potent and powerful. Affirmations can be made more powerful by:

1. Frequency of repetition.
2. Regularity of repetition.
3. Clarity in wording of the affirmation which must be consistent with physical and spiritual law.
4. Maintaining consistency in the wording of the affirmation.
5. Physical relaxation during affirmation practice to deepen the access to the subconscious mind and the spiritual stream of divine consciousness. In the states of consciousness associated with falling asleep, waking, restless sleep, or states of deep relaxation, the repetition of affirmations will bring greater results. This will allow a deeper

absorption into the unconscious mind and allow greater penetration and entering into the spiritual stream of consciousness.

When using affirmations, we repeat the same basic idea or content for an extended period of time. We dilute their power by continuously rewording, reworking, or changing themes.

Important Note: An affirmation should be stated in **Present Time**, as if it is currently materializing or has already manifested. A statement of future results essentially issues a command to our divine self and subconscious mind to **delay** manifestation. To indicate future benefit, or future improvement, is to order both the unconscious and the spiritual stream to cease making changes in the Now. Now is all there is in reality.

For example, stating "I will soon be well" or "Positive circumstances will soon be materializing," sends a powerful message of delayed results. The Now then stagnates. Ideas expressed for fruition in the future are always restrictive and limit present change. That is why affirmations are stated in the present tense: I am well now.

Spiritualized Affirmations

Few books adequately address the true power of affirmations. One exception is Paramahansa

Yogananda's *Scientific Healing Affirmations*. In order for affirmations to change one's life, they must be accompanied by the sincerity to strive for greater self-knowledge. That being said, most people do not understand that they have one of the most powerful tools for change right within them. When language is infused with the repeated vibration of truth in Spirit, another level of universal power is unleashed.

As our spiritualized language affirms, our words create an energy blueprint that has the power of vibrational attraction, operating through the law of magnetism and the law of attraction. As mentioned earlier in this chapter, these grooves create energy channels that are deepened by repetition, allowing for a precise, highly-charged flow of energy in motion to move along existing neural highways. This then attracts similar and like vibration: "Like attracts like." Energy seeks its own level. Energy blueprints cannot evaluate the truth or falsehood of the ideas. True and false alike can be imprinted. It is the persistent application of positive thought and word over time that allows for a shift to greater positive magnetism in life.

Will-directed thoughts, charged with the spiritual power of intention, are catalysts for change. Words infused with spiritual truth, whether or not we believe that truth, will create energized grooves that allow for a greater access of Spirit.

When affirmations, along with other positive spiritual practices including prayer and meditation, are combined with a willingness to journey into self-discovery, the result is a dramatic thrust forward in self-knowing. New levels of self-actualization occur. Powerful alignments happen when we ally ourselves first with truth and in divine intention to progress and claim our own true nature.

Not only are these wondrous events being accelerated through the practice of affirmation, but the Limited Self begins to move into closer alignment, connection, and attunement with its own higher nature, the Eternal Self. As the Limited Self begins communion with the essence of its own nature, we achieve greater access to our spiritual dimension while the ego-based consciousness becomes less dominant. That greater alignment creates the bridge over which we can journey toward true happiness. We can become true creators of deliberate happiness.

> *The power of affirmations allows for a new level of alignment and integration with the fragmented parts of the Limited Self.*

This is not a journey of faith or belief, for within each of us is the truth of knowing our own nature. Accessing that nature is the ultimate human struggle and goal. Words spoken in truth that contain Spirit beckon man homeward to the highest place of his self-knowing.

Other affirmations may seek material benefits, worldly possessions and greater abundance. Yet many books on affirmations rightly caution "you need to be careful what you wish for!" We must ask ourselves whether we desire alignment with our highest good. Does our desire come at the expense of others in a manner that is not harmonious with the good intentions of our selves or the universal flow? Will receiving what we affirm further anchor us in the Limited Self and the world of the senses? Or will we move toward the Eternal Self that is ever beckoning us?

The championing of instant gratification, supporting our expansion into the material world and its pleasures, is ultimately self-defeating in our quest for happiness.

As noted earlier, deeper journeys into introspection are necessary to achieve lasting happiness. Applying will, determination, and proper spiritual intention in affirmations may not sound appealing; but to achieve the levels of joy and contentment we seek, we must engage will, patient determination and spiritual intention. Doing so may also require us to challenge our assumptions, reframe our values and consciously contemplate aspects of our self and nature.

Individuals and the Divine Source do have the power to materialize abundance. But if affirmations are used only for greater material gain, then we may lose the opportunity for permanent, transcendent happiness. We may delay the self-knowing that brings joy.

Spiritual affirmations use words and ideas which contain spiritual truth. The vibration of God and creation resonates in sound energy throughout the universe. This spiritual truth vibrates at a different, higher vibratory rate than mundane language. When we express and resonate with the vibration of spiritual truth, the spiritual reality of our own nature is energized and our knowing is further awakened. The sound-vibration of spiritual truth resonates in the ether and words become divine embodiments of thought, a pathway to inner remembrance of our own nature. Our deeply-held desire for happiness is a summons to come to that place of joy, the site of the true essence of our soul nature.

Affirmations aligned with spiritual truth have an intense power to open the door of new possibilities and allow us to become powerful creators in the universe, for that is our inherent nature. That is our destiny. These techniques, including the repetition of spiritualized affirmations, can take us to new levels of mastery and understanding. We exist as a force in creation itself. The direction of that force is best determined by the alignment and expression of our connection with one another, with nature, and with God.

> *Nothing materializes separate from Spirit-- even if our perception fails to recognize the connection.*

Affirmations that are spiritually-based are inherently different from those which express wants, needs, or desires in the physical-material world. A hypothesis of this book is that spiritualized affirmations will yield an entirely different level of favorable results than affirmations based primarily on desires tied to the physical-material reality.

An example of an affirmation on abundance or prosperity may be "I have wealth and riches in my life. Wealth is mine. A new house is manifesting for me." When that affirmation is stated in this manner, the house is seen as the ultimate end and goal. *The material object is seen as the Source which provides something.* The language does not express a connection to an idea, or concept of Spirit behind the manifestation, or one that includes man as a participant in that manifestation. That which finally materializes in physical manifestation must begin its journey from the realm of ideas, thoughts, and energy. There is a Source from which ideas, thoughts and energy flow.

Spirit does not follow the laws of man's perception, but expresses the reality of itself. Hopefully

31

we will be mindful to have our desires reflect our highest nature and the spiritual truth that there is nothing in creation and nothing in the realm of desire that is separated from our journey as spiritual beings operating in a material world.

The Importance of Conscious Language in Affirmations

Any affirmation that is preceded with the words "I Am" is making a spiritual statement. "I Am" refers directly to the name of God, who is beyond all names. "I Am the I Am" may be thought of as a name of God. When we say, "I Am (anything)," we are stating that the God within us is in that circumstance or situation. The use of the words "I Am" in affirmation should be clearly stated with the proper spiritual intention. Pure spiritual intention is always harmonized with spiritual truth.

> *"Thoughts are things."*
> -Edgar Cayce

The affirmation *"I am wealthy and prosperous"* is a very different affirmation from this one: *"Money and wealth are mine."* When there is a statement "I Am" it is a statement of the God-aspect in man. In that expressed statement, there comes to be another level of alignment, a vibration with man in creation and man in manifestation. Instead of stating *"A new house is manifesting for me,"* affirm: *"I am one with the Eternal Source of all creation. I am one with the abundant supply of that Divine force that is ever-creating abundance and prosperity in my life Now."* (This affirmation could be separated into two parts if desired.) When the affirmation is stated in this manner, there is recognition of the Eternal Source, the highest source of creation, the Divine Source of all life. By recognizing that Source we draw closer to alignment with It, synchronizing the vibratory energy that is within ourselves and outside of ourselves in creation.

> We need to be careful not to limit the concept of prosperity from the Divine Source itself.

We would do well not to limit our ideas of prosperity to the materialization of one or more specific items. For example, to believe that you are prosperous based on the sudden appearance of a new house limits you and improperly measures the stream of positive possibilities. We must take care not to limit the concept of prosperity mandating from the Divine Source itself.

The Spiritual Source is the supplier of all. Affirmations which directly, or indirectly, affirm that truth will generate a greater access to the Source itself. To believe our possibilities are limited in any way, is to negate the truth of our being a receiver from the Eternal well-spring of all-giving, all-supply, and all-life. In the statement, *"Money and wealth are mine,"* wealth again is seen as the source of the manifestation. Such an affirmation does not recognize the opportunity for co-creation with Spirit. The ego-identified man becomes the primary focus of manifestation, separate from Spirit, whereas properly formulated affirmations acknowledge that wealth is a direct manifestation or by-product of that Eternal Source.

As we deepen our practice of affirmation, we may become aware of certain contrary beliefs. If we affirm greater expression of creativity, but our self-dialogue and interior thought process associates creativity with financial need, then our results will be diminished. Any thought that implies "creativity cannot generate financial success for me" minimizes the possibility of financial success through creative and artistic work. Creativity paired with the idea of lack will always, by the law of magnetic attraction, create a state of lack. Even so we should affirm that prosperity and creativity may be powerfully paired. Over time, our affirmation will help us see that creative expression and financial success may be achieved simultaneously.

Why Do Affirmations "Fail"?

Sometimes people who have tried to use valid and inspiring affirmations for higher goals report, usually after a limited period of time and sporadic efforts, that affirmations do not work. In such cases, the fault usually lies in the practice and attitude of the practitioner. Perhaps our suspicion that they will fail becomes part of our self-talk and thus is unconsciously affirmed, so the words operate in reverse of our desired intention. Energy follows thought and energized thought manifests materialization in kind.

Success with affirmations requires becoming aware of these patterns. Only then can we change negative themes to positive ones. Then we become dynamic co-creators with dynamic intention, will, imagination, and visualization to manifest our dreams into reality. Affirmations require patience, faith, concentration, proper practice, surrender and alignment with Divine will to reach their full potential. As Paramahansa Yogananda wrote in his inspiring *Scientific Healing Affirmations*, "Words saturated with sincerity, conviction, faith, and intuition are like highly explosive vibratory bombs, which, when set off, shatter the rocks of difficulties and create the change desired." (p. 4)

How to Practice Affirmations

There are different times to practice, such as:
- Formal waking state.
- Informal waking state.
- Relaxed state.

Technique:
1. **Decide on your affirmation(s).** Determine, and write down, which affirmation(s) you will be repeating. You may vary from this initial plan, but mentally place your intention on what you desire to affirm. Proceed with sincerity of purpose and certainty that the creative force will become super-charged by your acts of mental repetition and your regularity and consistency of practice.
2. **Proper posture.** The spine should be erect. You may sit in a straight-back chair, in a relaxed posture, but the spine should be erect and the chin level with the floor. The feet should remain flat on the ground.
3. **Intention of protection** – this both enhances the practice and creates a greater alignment with Spirit.
    a. Begin with an affirmation of protection, stated mentally or out loud. The intention to call on the spiritual force should always precede the practice of affirmation. An example of a protection affirmation is this: "In the Name, through the Power, and by the Word of (name of divinity), a wall of living flame is built around and about me and I give thanks for this great protection Now." This affirmation is from a former Franciscan monk and a

direct disciple of Paramahansa Yogananda, John Laurence.

b. Visualizing white light around oneself, or another person(s), will intensify our connection to the spiritual force and energetically send forth this positive energy toward another. Visualizing white light may be accomplished by mentally tracing the idea of white light around the body, or visualizing a spherical, egg-shape pattern, making certain that the white light also is completed around both the head and the feet. It is not by your power to see or visualize white light, or see colors around another person that brings forth a response; it is your vibrations of good intention that summons the love vibration in a manner that brings forth the energy of blessings for yourself or for another.

4. **Formal affirmation practice.** Take the list of affirmations that you have chosen and start with affirmation number two (the first one always being for protection). If possible, state the affirmation out loud. Never repeat by rote, but concentrate on the meaning, intention, and the thought expressed by the words and sentences. Restate the affirmation 4-6 times. Then decrease the volume with approximately the same number of repetitions. Continue through several stages until you are at a

whisper level, and then culminate this practice of affirmations by a mental repetition, using the same approximate number of repetitions each time.

5. **Then proceed to the next affirmation** following with the same pattern.

An excellent discussion and instruction on the practice of affirmations, as well as a list of potent spiritualized affirmations is to be found in:
Scientific Healing Affirmations
by Paramahansa Yogananda.
This publication is available online through Self-Realization Fellowship at http://www.yogananda-srf.org/ and at many bookstores.

Informal Waking State Practice

You may do affirmations with a less formalized technique by simply mentally or verbally repeating the affirmations off and on throughout the day while sitting or while active. However, if you combine both the more formal technique and also utilize the informal practice, you will greatly accelerate the results.

State of Relaxation or Pre-sleep Practice

Affirmations may be effectively done prior to sleep or upon awakening from sleep. In this state, you may mentally duplicate the pattern of affirmation practice. Do each affirmation with focused concentration a number of times, simply repeating them mentally. After a series of repetitions, move from one affirmation to another, but always begin with the protection affirmation.

Note: After affirmation practice, you may want to do an affirmation concluding, *"My affirmations are producing powerful and positive results in my life Now."*

Affirmations Regarding Family of Origin

The following affirmation is recommended for individuals who have issues around negative parental energy earlier in their life: *"I give thanks for I Am a divine child of God. I Am divinely loved and divinely loving. I give thanks for I Am loved **unconditionally** by the Heavenly Father. I give thanks for I Am loved **unconditionally** by the Divine Mother."* Repeat each sentence twice.

Please note in these affirmations the "I Am" statements. "I Am" is the name of God. When we say "I am unloved," we are stating the God force within us is in a state of being unloved. When we say "I am unlovable," we are misstating the truth of our essence. The truth is, God is the very Source of love. God resides within each individual, so nothing is outside the embrace of that Love. The ideas "I am unloved" and "I am unlovable" are, in fact, spiritual error. Love is the source which brought us all into manifestation. Love is our nature and the expression of God within us.

This affirmation makes reference to a personified aspect of God as father figure or as mother figure. The repetition of this concept begins to defuse the themes around one's inability to access parental love. What was not achieved in childhood will never be achieved by simply replaying the themes of that childhood. More understanding may be gained about how it affected us, but the feelings of disconnection, the lack of love or support, or the emotional unavailability of a parent will not be changed by simply replaying the record of the past. As one repeats the Divine love affirmation, given above, with consistency and constancy, one begins to access another level of that energy stream, the basis of which is the unconditional love of the Divine Force. This affirmation has given great comfort and a new self-definition, along with an increased capacity to love, and to be loved, to many people. Despite extensive therapy, many people were unable to satisfactorily deal with father and mother issues from childhood. However, they achieved remarkable results after learning this affirmation technique. It is highly recommended for those who have unresolved parental issues, and for those interested in

> *It is our inherent right and the promise of God that if we seek, so shall we find, and in finding, so we shall claim.*

40

the voyage of discovery around integrating more of the Eternal Self.

Chapter Three

Affirmations Change Consciousness

You are invited to employ affirmations to achieve the highest good and to attain lasting fulfillment by understanding your highest expression and your higher purpose.

Spiritualized, power-charged affirmations assist us in personal empowerment by transforming consciousness, eradicating negative thoughts and lessening the power of negative self-talk.

Key Topics Addressed in This Chapter:

- Increase your expertise in identifying core negative thoughts that can be largely eradicated by the application of affirmations.
- How affirmations lessen the power of negative self-talk.
- How *spiritualized affirmations* increase your success in personal empowerment by the power of true transformation of consciousness.

- How to create and power-charge your own spiritualized affirmations.

Energized Ideas Create Fields of Attraction

False ideas, if they are repeated and energized, take on a life of their own. Whether we know it or not, they create their own core energy to attract conditions and circumstances into our lives. Unconsciously we may already be affirming negative thoughts and getting unforeseen and unwished-for results. My intention is to convey a clear understanding of how affirmations affect every aspect of life so that one may achieve the highest good and attain lasting fulfillment. Toward this aim, we must also understand that affirmations may be used in ways that are contrary to our highest expression and our higher purpose. Perhaps we are using negative self-talk as affirmations, not recognizing the power of words, or how energy clusters around stated ideas.

These negative results occur when we:

- Make circular negative statements about ourselves.
- Say negative statements that limit outcomes.
- Repeat fatalistic statements about our life and circumstances.
- Project our negative anticipation of others' behaviors.

If you are uncertain about the power and validity of affirmations, then I would encourage you to identify any one negative thought or negative self-assessment that you have often repeated to yourself. When you mentally say to yourself, *"I am unworthy of being truly loved,"* or *"No matter how hard I try I will never be successful,"* or *"in the end, everything I attempt to accomplish is taken away from me,"* you are using powerful affirmations, but as a negative, devaluing judgment of yourself.

We simply don't identify such repeated negative statements as affirmations. We see them as simple thoughts and ideas, little realizing their power, or how they are charged by potent energy. We are affirming the opposite of that which we want. We are unknowingly underestimating the tremendous creative power of our minds.

Attempt to identify five negative thoughts, or statements of negative self-assessment, that you repeat with regularity. The truth is we all talk with ourselves in some form of negative self-dialogue or negative self-assessment, perhaps forgetting how powerful that language and those feeling states really are. When we sustain a negative internal dialogue, we are practicing an affirmation technique, but these ideas are, in fact, negative affirmations. Hopefully, you have not become a master of negative affirmations, which are disguised as negative self-talk. Such repeated negative affirmations, even if unconscious, operate according to the same spiritual laws. Our own ideas and energy-charged affirmations can work for us or against us, in our pursuit of happiness. Our goal is to use affirmations in a way that enhances our lives and dynamically transforms us.

We Tend to Believe Our Own Thoughts

Over a lifetime we become so used to our own thoughts that we no longer differentiate between what is real and unreal, true and false. Our use of negative self-statements may be perceived as practical or realistic. We may think such negative statements are accurate self-evaluations. We may even perceive stated negativity as an indication of humility. *"I am a sinner, unworthy to be in the holy presence of God"* is in stark contrast to an idea such as *"I am a divine child of God, loved and loving in that divine presence."* It's clear which affirmation

> The word "discernment" will be used here to signify the power to discriminate between a perceived reality and the possibility that the perception may be illusory. Discernment is not the same as faith, for faith may be a personal creation, either mental or emotional, but discernment is a quite certain recognition of the reality or truth of something, and is acquired by the higher consciousness.
>
> Isha Lubicz, *Opening of the Way: A Practical Guide to the Wisdom of Ancient Egypt*

allows us to embrace more of our self in a divine relationship with God.

There are those who feel that it is blasphemy to think of themselves in any terms other than a sinner, fallen from Grace. This is not to challenge how a person wishes to live a religious life, but rather to suggest that affirming a divine connection of love with the Creator, may expand possibilities of a greater relationship with God and a more satisfying spiritual life.

We may be unaware that regularly-repeated negative self-statements may be a continuation and duplication of childhood themes in image and potent language. We may cloak negative ideas as being realistic perceptions about our circumstances and the realism of life. These thought patterns diminish God's possibilities for our life. We repeat them in a manner often completely unaware that we are creating our present and future reality with these powerful, mental projections. We are limiting the definition of our Self and the very expression of the essence of who we are. We must unlock the prison of our negative self-definitions and release ourselves to the daylight of new possibilities.

> *Keys of new creation through affirmation have been lovingly placed in our hands.*

We will not claim and harness that power until we begin to reflect upon some of the potential of that power which we possess. The great and true message is we are capable of shifting and changing feeling states and accessing the greater good by implementation of specific spiritual principles in combination with our energized will to succeed. Energy and focus applied with regularity and sufficient repetition of affirmations, aligned with truth, have the power to destroy negative constellations of energy. It may become a powerful vehicle to claiming that Eternal Self we have intuitively known but were unable to access. That Self has been hidden by false delusive statements of our minds and insufficient awareness of our spiritual essence.

Self-dialogue Provides a Clue

To create a new definition of self, to achieve different and more positive circumstances, and/or a deeper connection with God and our spiritual life, then we must affirm only that which we want to manifest.

To effectively employ affirmation techniques we must gain clarity about our own thought processes and self-dialogue. What is our habitual trend of thought? Is our self-dialogue primarily negative or is it primarily positive? Do we see ourselves as an optimist or a pessimist? Are we similar or dissimilar in our mental approaches to those who raised us?

One of the best ways to answer these questions is to observe our self-dialogue during emotional upsets or difficult trials in our lives. What are the themes that tend to repeat themselves? If we feel unloved, do we tell ourselves that something must be wrong with us? Do we ever say to ourselves that we are unlovable or incapable of loving others? Do we feel unworthy of being loved? Do we feel unworthy of success? What repetitive ideas that drive our self-dialogue? Possibilities include:

- **Our aloneness in the world.**
- **Our inability to achieve deep, continuing connection with others.**
- **Our unlovable or unloving nature.**
- **Our inability to create lasting, positive change.**
- **Our powerlessness over life.**

Repetition of ideas increases the energized force field of thought. That energy does not remain static, but is a moving life force operating through the law of similar attraction. This magnetized affirmation has great potency and the capacity to finally materialize the statement of intention. The power of dynamic energy directed by the mind is an expression of the life force. We are co-creators unfolding the cosmic force of

> *Affirmations work, not because of the belief in that which is being stated, but by the power of repetition that becomes charged with dynamic creative force.*

48

divine manifestation; we do this with language, thought, intention, imagination, and with the power of will-directed activity.

Affirmation Technique to Destroy Core Negative Thoughts

1. Identify core negative thoughts. What are the dominant themes replayed in times of real crisis? Examining negative self-statements is a powerful tool toward unearthing dominant themes. These thought forms are then exposed to the light of day, to the light of Spirit.
2. After identifying the core negative themes or self-statements, write them down in a journal or notebook. This is extremely helpful in our efforts to become more aware of themes that have come out in therapy or self-help exploration, and to identify what negative self-talk still needs to be uprooted.
3. Next, substitute a positive affirmation which is in direct opposition to the negative self-statement you have been making. Eliminate the negative statement by replacing it with a positive one. For example, a negative theme such as being unworthy of love ("I am unloved and unlovable") can be counteracted with a positive affirmation like "I am divinely loved and an instrument for the Divine expression of love to others."

4. The affirmation needs to resonate with spiritual truth to achieve its potential. The greater the resonance the more effective it will be. The power of repetition correlates with our ability to manifest results.

Spiritual Affirmations Can Transform Consciousness

We can make our minds so like still water that beings gather about us that they may see, it may be, their own images and so live for a moment with a clearer perhaps even with a fiercer life because of our quiet.
                    William Butler Yeats, Irish poet

Deep down we all desire the peace of still waters. But when the personality aspect of the Limited Self drives our lives, we are less centered in our soul nature or Eternal Self. Since it is neither possible nor desirable to obliterate the human experience that shapes our individuality, we do not wish to eliminate the Limited Self, but rather to achieve a progressively stronger alignment, interplay, exchange, and participation with our higher soul nature. That nature is Spirit – perfect in being, absolute in truth, and joyous in existence. Consciously or unconsciously we all long to find that Home again. Deep down we do desire to make our minds like still water, calm in the certainty of divine love and perfected self-knowing. In that claiming we know fully who we are and what we are—divine children of God who may have lost sight of the magnificent vision of ourselves and one another.

As noted in this and earlier chapters, an affirmation used as a spiritualized technique must contain spiritual truth in idea and in the language expressing that idea. To state, "I am a Martian from Mars. I am a bird, a cat, or a dog," will never change our nature no matter how powerful our intention or our capacity to visualize.

Similarly, one cannot state an affirmation that includes the idea, "I am *not.*" "I Am" will always respond to its God name. And we may be energizing very false statements by the attempt to place a negative "not, don't, can't, won't" after the "I Am" statement. When we affirm, *"I am love, I am light,"* we are stating the truth of our soul nature, rather than expressing an aspect of personality.

We are claiming, affirming, and properly energizing the truth of our nature in that spiritual affirmation. So our goal is to affirm in these "I am" statements only that which exists in purity and perfection as an attribute or aspect of Spirit.

If we listen, we can note how often negative statements are used in everyday language: "I am inadequate, unlovable, unsuccessful, not creative, not talented, undeserving, a sinner, a failure, loser." Those references, or similar types of judgments, are then extended to others. Such negative statements are simply not true of the Eternal Selves.

The affirmation, *"I am light, I am love"* states the essence of our nature, which exists in absolute truth. When such truth is intoned, the vibratory energy of spirit gains the power to become alive, evermore, in creation. Our words call on God to reveal Himself and it is in this revelation of ourselves that we discover God.

For this reason, it is important that we continue intoning such spiritual statements of truth with willed intention and regularity. Constantly changing the words and ideas and content of affirmations does not allow for a deeper penetration from the conscious to the unconscious, and from there, into the God conscious stream.

Affirmations can help to break pernicious habits, but only if they are invested with the power of dynamic will and are phrased properly. If someone has the habit of smoking, it's most effective to affirm oneself as free of all bad habits, avoiding any words that conjure images of the specific habit. An affirmation which visualizes the smoking behavior will strengthen the compulsive aspect of the addiction energy. In this instance, a beneficial affirmation is, *"I give thanks for I am free of all bad habits. Daily my power of dynamic will strengthens. I am powerful in the expression of my will and dynamic intention."*

Never under any circumstances visualize the habit to be broken, for by visualizing it, the habit becomes re-energized. Instead, imagine the growing power of your own dynamic will and visualize that you are completely free, have no bondage whatsoever, not even in the thoughts, mental concepts or language of the affirmation.

Affirmations Work with Precision

Affirmations are a tool that allow for the transformation of consciousness. As such, the more specific we are in our affirmation, the greater it can penetrate and uproot the cause of our difficulty. We are not on a quest for superficial change. We are proceeding on a deeply-committed course to discover who we are. It makes sense, then, to strengthen and utilize this potent technique, or any other, that will allow greater integration of the ego-based personality and the higher self.

When our consciousness begins to transform, we view the possibilities of greater power and greater opportunity within us. Affirmations, when properly repeated, are the intonation of God knowledge, of God's vibratory energy. They are a distillation of Spirit, manifesting as Sound, creating an awakening of consciousness, leading some day to Cosmic consciousness.

Because man tends to be ignorant of his soul, Paramahansa Yogananda writes, "human consciousness is isolated from Cosmic Consciousness. The mind of man is subject to change and limitation, but Cosmic Consciousness is free from all restrictions and is never involved in experiences of duality (death and life, disease and health, fleeting sorrow and fleeting joy)...the process of liberating human consciousness consists in training it by study, affirmations, concentration, and meditation...." (p.34 *Scientific Healing Affirmations.*) We have already begun this process of liberating human consciousness; continuing to train ourselves in techniques of affirmation and meditation will turn our attention away from the mind's endless fluctuations of thought and emotion and toward the subtler and more stable vibrations of our higher selves and higher consciousness.

Creating Your Own Affirmations

In Chapter Two, we saw that to be effective, each affirmation must be aligned with spiritual truth, consistent with physical and spiritual law, and clear in its wording. We also underscored the importance of frequency and regularity of repetition of the affirmation and we have seen the absolute necessity for each affirmation to be stated positively and to never mention any bad habit to be eradicated.

But affirmations are also more easily remembered, repeated and power-charged if the statement is in words and rhythms congenial to you as an individual. For instance, younger people may not identify with certain words and uses of language. They may prefer shorter affirmations and more brisk rhythms because of their own musical taste for hip-hop or other forms of contemporary music. That is fine and as it should be. In fact, the musicality of an affirmation can be an aid to memory.

Similarly, older people or those brought up in a religious environment may prefer affirmations that use the more archaic vocabulary and rhythms of traditional prayer. Still others may want the content of the affirmation to reflect their belief in a certain savior, prophet, goddess or wise woman – or their reverence for all religions. The Affirmation for Protection by John Laurence, for instance, can be tailored to each person's belief system, or it can reflect a tolerance of all by including several holy sources in the phrase – "In the **Name**, through the **Power** / And by the **Word** of Jesus the Christ, Yogananda, Buddha, Mohammed, and all the Great Ones...."

Those who work with mantras and more ancient icons of divinity and wisdom might wish to reformulate a mantra as an affirmation. Instead of bowing to the icon, the present tense affirmation might say, "Through the love and by the power of Saraswati, my creative work flowers Now." (Saraswati is the Indian goddess of sacred and secular wisdom and the arts.) Or, "The Divine Mother loves me unconditionally: I feel her warm embrace Now."

The larger point is that affirmations will be more readily employed, memorized, spoken and repeated if the phrasing, imagery and rhythm of the words feels right for the practitioner.

Conclusion: Claim Your Self

Having read here about the what, how and why of affirmations, you are now invited to power-charge your life. Whenever you are on the path to change, you can begin to recreate your patterns of thought and action with affirmations.

What stands in the way of your claiming your power? If lack of belief is the cause, then know that belief in your power without effort will prevent you from claiming the prize of your true self.

What stands in the way of your happiness? One primary cause is your desire that life will in some way be different, but it will only be different if you change your circumstances when possible—and if you change your consciousness, even if it looks impossible. Your habits in consciousness are the greatest deterrent to your claiming happiness and discovering the powerful depths of yourself.

Wherever you are in your life, take the power journey of self-discovery and personal claiming. If you start now with the practice of affirmations, you will discover that you are an alchemist who can change your thoughts. *You* are the creator who creates with the greatness of yourself and merges with the creation of all life, with all that is.

AFFIRM YOUR POWER
You are an expression
Of the power of the universe.
You are a divine expression
of the thought of God.

Thought is the
Creative substance of all.
Change your thoughts;
Power-charge your life.

Chapter Four

An Anthology of Spiritually Based Affirmations

The preceding chapters presented a number of affirmations on spiritual themes, always to be repeated with dynamic will and intention. By systematically repeating truths contained in Spirit, we lay claim to our inherent power to co-create with the Divine. Energized, spiritually-based affirmations unleash a flow of positive energy in our lives.

Gathered below is a sampler of affirmations on themes of Enhancing Our Spirituality, Integrating the Dual Nature of Man, Manifestation, Abundance and Prosperity, Health and Wholeness, and Creativity. The larger edition of *Deliberate Happiness: Practical Steps To An Empowered Life* contains hundreds of affirmations on these and many more themes. I hope some of these will resonate with you as you make affirmations a part of your daily practice.

Protection Affirmation

In the **Name**, through the **Power**
And by the **Word** of (name of divinity),
A wall of living flame is built around and about me
And I give thanks for this great protection Now.
                                        --John Laurence
(A wall of living flame refers to the "white light" or the Holy Spirit.)

To Enhance Spirituality

For Divine Re-parenting
I am the Heavenly Father.
I am the Divine Mother.
They reside within me
and I reside within them.

For Becoming One With The Field of Light
I am divine light,
a shining diamond essence
of God.
I move as a force,
transforming the world
into a field of light.

For Support from Source
The force of my positive intention
for self-empowerment
is supported and guided
by the Source of All.

For Self-Claiming as God's Child
I align myself with Truth.
The power of creation
resides within me.
In sound and form
I claim my truth,
I affirm my being.
I affirm
I am a divine child of God.
I am divinity incarnate.

For Happiness and Peace Within
I affirm
the manifestation of the good,
happiness, peace, harmony
and greater attunement
to the source of All.

For Potent Co-creation
I am a co-creator
with Light,
Love, and Possibilities.

For Divine Union
I am enveloped
In the bliss waves of God.

For Ascending Toward the Divine
Arrow spine
point starward
pulsating lightwaves
thrust to ascension.

For Awakening in God
I give thanks
for I am awake in God NOW.
I ride the divine breath.
I ride the sacredness
of the sound Aum.

<u>For the Thundering Power of Om (Aum)</u>
Buffalo, thunderous hooves
ride the crashing waves.
All one
Thunderous Om
Lightning flash
Resounding sound
Calling home
Sacred Om
Sacred Om.

<u>For Tranquility</u>
I am tranquil.
I am serene.
I am serenity
embodied in
human form.
I am tranquil.
I am serene.

<u>For Direct Communication with the Divine</u>
I give thanks
for I am in an altered state
of direct communion
and direct experience
with the Divine
and my own sacred nature.

<u>For Divine Breath</u>
I give thanks
for I breathe
the breath of <u>Christ</u> (or <u>any other name of divinity</u>).

<u>For Complete Integration</u>
I give thanks
for the harmonious development
of my psychic and spiritual gifts and abilities
manifesting NOW.   --John Laurence

For Receptivity to Miracles
I give thanks to God
for through divine intercession
my consciousness is increasingly receptive
to the vibration of God and Spirit.
I give thanks for miracles occurring NOW.

For Floating in Peaceful Waters
In the waters of peace,
I reflect.
In the waters of peace,
I submerge.

For Saintliness
I personify the virtues
of saints
for I walk in their
footsteps.
In striving,
I become patient.
In emulation,
I become saintly.

For Divine Grace
I raise my heart
to Thee.
It is the sacrifice
and the gift of my loving.
Bestow Thy grace
of divine acceptance.

For Peaceful Self-Knowing
I sit on the throne of serenity.
I inhale the air of peace.
The crown of knowing
encircles my head.
I breathe the silence.

For Self Realization
I tread the sacred ground.
Each step moves me
to greater understanding.
Each step moves me
to greater realization.
I am realized NOW.

For Vibratory Attunement with Aum (Om)
In tune am I
with God
in vibration,
God in light,
God in sound,
for I ride the vibration
of the holy, sacred Aum.
(Amen may be used in place of "Aum.")

For God-like Perception and Wisdom
Lord God, Jehovah
You have bestowed
Thy wisdom.
You have endowed me
with perception.
By Thy grace,
I exercise that perception
to behold the One
in all.

For Coming Home to Om (Aum)
Sound of Om
call me home.
Sound of Om
call me home.

For Expansion in the Light
Streams of light
enter into the center of my mind.
My mind expands in all knowing.
My light expands in all being.

For Wisdom-based Vision
Through wisdom-based perception,
I see.
Through discernment,
I act.
Reason, wisdom, and discernment
are mine — NOW.

For Unconditional Bliss and Love
The Divine Source
is revealing Itself to me.
It is peace, joy, and bliss.
Unconditional Love surrounds me
NOW.

For Clarity to see God
Unfolding in ever-greater clarity
is the light of God,
leading me
to the face of myself
and to the heart of God.

For Knowing Divine Destiny

I am one with my destiny
of higher knowing.
I am one with my destiny
of God knowing.

For Peace in the Cool Waters
The cool waters of peace
bathe me.
I follow the breath ripples
of my mind.
The still waters
encircle me.
Peace is my own.
The cool waters of peace
bathe me
ever more.

Affirmations to Integrate Our Dual Nature: Eternal & Limited Selves

For Attunement With The Divine
Attuned, Aligned,
Integrated Self.
Content in Being,
Peaceful in Serenity,
Awake in Spirit.

For Joy-filled Knowing
Being in knowing
I am.
Joy-filled,
light-illuminated,
ever penetrated,
ever known.
Joy-filled bliss I am.
Joy-filled bliss I am.

For Aligning with Essence
Celestial Light,
align me with the truth
of my essence and the
power of Spirit.

For Interior Peace in the Divine
Clear perception is mine.
Contemplative awareness
is mine.
My Interiorized Consciousness
brings me peace.

For Beholding the Face of God
I behold the face of God.
I parted the curtains of penetration
and the face I saw
was my own.

For Self-Claiming Spirit in Nature
In becoming one
with nature
I claim my nature.
I am Spirit
in nature.

For Finding Self in Silence
In silence,
the seeker finds
himself.

For Mirroring The Divine Essence
Oh Lord, may I become less of myself
in ego-based consciousness
that I may become ever more one with Thee.
May I become truly a purified conduit
of Your love, of Your light, of Your grace.
May I become a perfected mirror
of the divine essence
which is You, Oh Lord.

For Empowerment in the Light
Radiant light
of possibilities,
I see the
inherent power
within me.
I claim the light.
I claim the possibilities.
I claim the power
of knowing myself.

For Receiving All
The eternal wellspring
of all giving,
of all creation,
and all life
bestows upon me
all giving,
all Light, and
all love.

For Attunement as a Child of God
I am a Divine Child of God.
I am awakening in God NOW.
Oh Lord, how may I be of service to You on this day!
Oh Lord, perfect my consciousness
that in perfect attunement and intuition
I may receive Your blessings.

Affirmations for Manifestation

For Harmonious Manifestation
Divine Source, Your desire
for me is manifesting.
It is harmonious
with my life purpose
and my higher self.

For the Cornucopia of Manifestation
The cornucopia
of all my desires overflows.
The bounty and the harvest
is ever greater in manifestation.
In the bounty I have discovered
my sole remaining desire
is to know Thee better.
That desire is now manifesting.

For Manifesting the Higher Good
I am attuned to the Divine will.
That which is for the higher good
is now manifesting.
In gratitude and reverence
I receive,
knowing that the bounty of love
and the bounty of God
is ever blessing me
in divine manifestation.

Affirmations for Prosperity and Abundance

For Abundance Through the Divine
My Father and I are One.
All things whatsoever the Father hath
are mine. (John 16:15)
I give thanks for the
abundance and prosperity
manifesting
in my life NOW.

For Abundance
I give thanks for
I am a magnet of success.
Doors of opportunity
are opening wide for me NOW.

For Material Abundance Manifesting
I give thanks for the great material abundance
manifesting in my life NOW.
Prosperity is my due!
Wealth is my claim!

For Harmony and Attunement to Limitless Supply
I am in harmonious balance
With the Divine and the Universe.
That Divine Source
is materializing ever-greater abundance,
prosperity and resources in my life NOW.
I attune to the Divine Source
in harmonious co-creation.
I am receiving from the limitless supply
of the Divine and the Universe NOW.

For Mining Unlimited Wealth
I am a miner of wealth,
A collector of translucent jewels.
I am a dispenser of the veins of gold.
Limitless is my supply
For I access
The riches of the heavens and the earth.

Affirmations for Healing and Wholeness

For Youthful Good Health
I am radiant, endless,
vibrant, electric energy and youth
in every cell and atom
of my being NOW.

-John Laurence

<u>For Healing and Claiming</u>
I am focusing
my intention and dynamic will
on this goal of total healing
with unbending purpose.
I am unstoppable
against any obstacle
that obstructs my power
of total healing
and total claiming.

<u>For Healing and Wholeness</u>
I am whole.
I am healed.
I am radiant in God's healing light.
I give thanks
for the miraculous healing of my body
NOW.

<u>For The Eternal Light of Healing</u>
That light eternal
destroys the vision
of sickness.
That light eternal
heals NOW.
(May add:)
I am healed NOW.
(or)_____(name of other person) is healed NOW.
(manifestation)

<u>For Healing Through the Light</u>
My flesh and body are light-filled.
My bones, blood, and organs
are revitalized
and energized.
I am a receiver of Grace.
I am healed by the light.

For Miraculous Healing NOW
I give thanks to God
for the miraculous healing
in all areas of my life:
the physical,
the mental,
the emotional,
the spiritual.
I give thanks
for the miraculous healing
in all areas of my life NOW.

For Wholeness and Health
All disease is removed
from my body NOW.
Only wholeness
and wellness
remain.
I claim my wellness NOW.

For Healing Breath
I am encircled
in the bubble of breath.
It contains my healing.
It contains my life force.
It contains my being.

For Divine Presence
I am fully present
with my divine self
in my physical form.

For Radiant Healing Energy
My physical form
is radiating
the energy of God.
My physical form
is rebalanced
by the healing
energy of God.

For Wholeness and Healing
I am fully present
in my wellness,
in my wholeness,
and in the energy field
within me.

For Healing Now in God's Light
I am healed NOW.
In gratitude
I acknowledge
I am healed NOW.
(Note above four paragraphs can be used together or apart.

I am Healed
I am healed.
I radiate God's
healing light.

For Divine Centering
I am in perfected alignment
with that Higher Self
of all knowing.
I am centered
in the light of divine healing.

For Miraculous Revitalization
I give thanks
for the miraculous healing
of my body NOW.
My body is revitalized
with the electrical flow to every cell.
The pranic force of the universe
energizes me,
heals me,
and recreates me.

For Miraculous Healing
I give thanks to God
for His miraculous healing
of my body NOW.
My body is revitalized
by the electrical flow to every cell.

Affirmations for Creativity

For Focus to Manifest Creativity
Night and day,
I am focused
in concentration.
My one-pointed focus
illumines all solutions
and dissolves all problems.
The power to create
is my birthright
manifesting.

For the Power to Create
The power to create
is expressing itself
through me.
Luminous possibilities
present themselves.
I capture the
thought bubbles
in my imagination.
My will-based initiative drives
the thought bubbles
into concrete manifestation.
Creativity shines,
reflecting
the luminous possibilities.

<u>For Creative Power in the Light</u>
I am the Light
of all suns.
I possess the power
of all creations.
My name is the name
of all Light,
all suns,
all power,
and all creations.

<u>For Infinite Creative Possibilities</u>
Abundance
and ever-new creativity
are mine NOW,
expressing with infinite possibilities.

<u>Blessings Abound</u>
I contemplate.
I see and penetrate
into unceasing
and unending
blessings.
I bow in gratitude
and appreciation.
I stand tall
In accepting all blessings.

Affirmations For Breaking Bad Habits

<u>For Strength to Severe Bad Habits</u>
The chains of bad habits
are severed and dismantled.
The power of choice remains.
I am emboldened
and strengthened
in my power
to choose courage
and even-mindedness.

<u>For Will to Be Free</u>
I give thanks
for I am permanently free
of all bad habits.
My power of dynamic will
is energized and strengthened.

<u>For Freedom From Bad Habits</u>
I give thanks for I am free of all bad habits.
Daily my power of dynamic will strengthens.
I am powerful in the expression
of my will and dynamic intention.

Chapter Five

Thoughts for the Day: A Sampler

Your life can be enriched and empowered by adding a positive, powerful thought to your daily practice of affirmations. The following thoughts are taken from a variety of sources worldwide. Some may appeal to you. And, of course, you may discover your own thought for the day in your own reading or experience.

As the mind and the feelings are directed inward, you begin to feel God's joy. The pleasures of the senses do not last; but the joy of God is everlasting. It is incomparable!
                              Paramahansa Yogananda

A bird does not sing because it has an answer. It sings because it has a song.
                                      Chinese Proverb

Life should be chiefly service. Without that ideal, the intelligence that God has given you is not reaching out toward its goal. When in service you forget the little self; you will feel the big Self of Spirit.
Paramahansa Yogananda

Let your hopes, not your hurts, shape your future.
Robert H. Schuller

Attachment is blinding; it lends an imaginary halo of attractiveness to the object of desire.
Sri Swami Yukteswar

This is my simple religion. There is no need for temples; no need for complicated philosophy. Our own brain, our own heart is our temple; the philosophy is kindness.
His Holiness, the Dalai Lama

A single footstep will not make a path on the earth, so a single thought will not make a pathway in the mind. To make a deep physical path, we walk again and again. To make a deep mental path, we must think over and over the kind of thoughts we wish to dominate our lives.
Henry David Thoreau

To the mind that is still, the whole universe surrenders.
Lao Tzu

We can make our minds so like still water that beings gather about us that they may see, it may be, their own images and so live for a moment with a clearer, perhaps even with a fiercer life because of our quiet.
W. B. Yeats

The laughter of the infinite God must vibrate through your smile. Let the breeze of His love spread your smiles in the hearts of men. Their fire will be contagious.
Paramahansa Yogananda

The fullness of joy is to behold God in everything.
Julian of Norwich

Today I will factor in uncertainty as an essential ingredient of my experience. In my willingness to accept uncertainty, solutions will spontaneously emerge out of the problem; out of the confusion and chaos will come order. The more uncertain things seem to be, the more secure I will feel, because uncertainty is my path to freedom. Through the wisdom of uncertainty, I will find my security.
Deepak Chopra

The ocean refuses no river.
Vedic Wisdom

As rivers flow into the sea, losing their individuality, so the enlightened, no longer bound by name and form, merge with the infinite, the radiant Cosmic Being.
Brihadaranyaka Upanishad

Faith is a bird that feels dawn breaking and sings while it is still dark.
Rabindranath Tagore

Everything you see has its roots in the unseen world. The forms may change, yet the essence remains the same. Every wonderful sight will vanish, every sweet word will fade, but do not be disheartened. The source they come from is eternal, growing, branching out giving new life and new joy. Why do you weep? The source is within you and this whole world is springing up from it.
The Sufi poet, Jalal ad-Din Muhammad Rumi

Forget what hurt you in the past, but never forget what it taught you.
Anonymous

When you sit in the silence of deep meditation, joy bubbles up from within, roused by no outer stimulus. The joy of meditation is overwhelming. Those who have not gone into the silence of true meditation do not know what real joy is.
Paramahansa Yogananda

*If you want others to be happy, practice compassion.
If you want to be happy, practice compassion.*
His Holiness, the 14th Dalai Lama

Blaming never helps. When you plant lettuce, if it does not grow well you don't blame the lettuce. You look into the reasons it is not doing well. ...Yet if we have problems with our friends or our family, we blame the other person. But if we know how to take care of them, they will grow like lettuce. ...No blame, no reasoning, no argument, just understanding. If you understand, and you show that you understand, you can love, and the situation will change.
Thich Nhat Hanh, Peace Is Every Step

Walk with those seeking truth... RUN FROM THOSE WHO THINK THEY'VE FOUND IT.
Deepak Chopra

Many people excuse their own faults but judge others harshly. We should reverse this attitude by excusing others' shortcomings and by harshly examining our own.
Paramahansa Yogananda

Understand that the past cannot and will not take you down. If it didn't then, it certainly can't now.
Unknown

*Are you jealous of the ocean's generosity?
Why would you refuse to give this joy to anyone?
Fish don't hold the sacred liquid in cups!
They swim the huge fluid freedom.*
Rumi

We need to find God, and he cannot be found in noise and restlessness. God is the friend of silence. See how nature—trees, flowers, grass—grow in silence. See the stars, the moon and the sun, how they move in silence...We need silence to be able to touch souls.
Mother Teresa

Before enlightenment: chop wood, carry water. After enlightenment: chop wood, carry water.
Zen Buddhist Proverb

You pray in your distress and in your need; would that you might pray also in the fullness of your joy and in your days of abundance.
Kahlil Gibran

The way of love is not a subtle argument.
The door there is devastation.
Birds make great sky-circles of their freedom.
How do they learn it? They fall, and falling, they're given wings.
Rumi

We are what we think. All that we are arises with our thoughts. With our
thoughts we make our world.
Gautama Buddha

Sometimes, simply by sitting, the soul collects wisdom.
Zen Proverb

Reading about nature is fine, but if a person walks in the woods and listens carefully, he can learn more than what is in books for the trees speak with the voice of God.
George Washington Carver

When it comes time to die, be not like those whose hearts are filled with the fear of death, so when their time comes they weep and pray for a little more time to live their lives over again in a different way. Sing your death song, and die like a hero going home.
    Mohican Chief Aupumut, 1725

When the ocean surges don't let me just hear it. Let it splash inside my chest.
    Rumi

Your vision will become clear only when you look into your heart. . .
Who looks outside, dreams.
Who looks inside, awakens.
    Carl Jung

You have to leave the city of your comfort and go into the wilderness of your intuition. What you will discover will be wonderful. What you will discover is yourself.
    Alan Alda

Each of us is here to discover our true Self...that essentially we are spiritual beings who have taken manifestation in physical form, that we're not human beings that have occasional spiritual experience, that we're spiritual beings that have occasional human experiences.
    Deepak Chopra

Follow your bliss. I say, follow your bliss and don't be afraid...and doors will open where you didn't know they were going to be. If you follow your bliss, doors will open for you that wouldn't have opened for anyone else.
    Joseph Campbell

You grow to heaven. You don't go to heaven.
    Edgar Cayce

The Great Spirit is in all things: he is in the air we breathe. The Great Spirit is our Father, but the earth is our mother. She nourishes us; that which we put into the ground she returns to us.
    Bedagi (Big Thunder), Wabanaki Algonquin

Live your beliefs and you can turn the world around.
    Henry David Thoreau

Holding on to anything is like holding on to your breath. You will suffocate. The only way to get anything in the physical universe is by letting go of it. Let go and it will be yours forever.
    Deepak Chopra

Re-examine all that you have been told. Dismiss what insults your soul.
    Walt Whitman

Do you want to be a power in the world? Then be yourself. Be true to the highest within your soul and then allow yourself to be governed by no customs or conventionalities or arbitrary man-made rules that are not founded on principle.
    Ralph Waldo Emerson

I have learned silence from the talkative, tolerance from the intolerant and kindness from the unkind. I should not be ungrateful to those teachers.
    Kahlil Gibran

Be with God, if He has taken from you that which you could never have imagined losing, and He will give you that which you could never have imagined owning.
    Shaykh Muḥammad Mutawallī al-Sharāwī

It is important to differentiate between your needs and your wants. Your needs are few, while your wants can be limitless. In order to find freedom and bliss, minister only to your needs. Stop creating limitless wants and pursuing the will-o'-the-wisp of false happiness.
                                    Paramahansa Yogananda

Am I not destroying my enemies when I make friends of them?
                                    Abraham Lincoln

If we could erase the "I's" and "mine's" from religion, politics, and economics, we should soon be free and bring heaven upon earth.
                                    Mahatma Gandhi

I am only one; but still I am one. I cannot do everything, but still I can do something; I will not refuse to do the something I can do.
                                    Helen Keller

Unselfishness is the governing principle in the law of prosperity.
                                    Paramahansa Yogananda

Never lose an opportunity of seeing anything that is beautiful; for beauty is God's handwriting — a wayside sacrament. Welcome it in every fair face, in every fair sky, in every fair flower, and thank God for it as a cup of blessing.
                                    Ralph Waldo Emerson

The first peace, which is the most important, is that which comes within the souls of people when they realize their relationship, their oneness with the universe and all its powers, and when they realize that at the center of the universe dwells the Great Spirit, and that this center is really everywhere, it is within each of us.
                                    Black Elk, Oglala Sioux

*Even after all this time
The sun never says to the earth,
"You owe Me."
Look what happens with a love like that,
It lights the whole sky.*

        Sufi mystic poet, Hafiz

Pride is blinding, banishing the vision of vastness possessed by greater souls. Humbleness is the open gate through which the divine flood of Mercy and Power loves to flow into receptive souls.

        Paramahansa Yogananda

www.ingramcontent.com/pod-product-compliance
Lightning Source LLC
Chambersburg PA
CBHW032022040426
42448CB00006B/704